The Littlest Shepherd

Ron Mehl, Jr.

Story and Illustrations by Sandy Gunderson

MULTNOMAH

Portland, Oregon

1 t was a cool, clear evening. The sun was just setting behind the faraway hills as the shepherds led their flock to the place where they were to spend the night. For the littlest shepherd, it had been a busy day. After waking up early, he had practiced with his slingshot, pulled briars from the sheeps' coats, and tried to learn them all by name.

ow the sun had fallen and the twinkling stars were making their journeys up to their places in the night sky. All the sheep were asleep, safe and sound. The littlest shepherd ate his supper and then sat down on a large, flat rock which was still warm from the day's sun. It was not long before the heat of the rock and the gentleness of the breeze lulled the shepherd boy to sleep.

"**W**ake up!" chided his grandfather, oldest and wisest of all the shepherds. "You must never fall asleep while you are watching the flock."

"But Grandfather," said the boy, stretching and rubbing the sleep from his eyes, "it has been such a long day and I am so very tired!"

"Grandson, let me tell you a story about a night just like tonight when I was a young shepherd just about your age. After what happened that night I never again fell asleep watching the flock," said the old shepherd with a twinkle in his eye.

"Once, when I was young and I was caring for the sheep with my father, I fell asleep on a bed of grass after a long day in the fields. But suddenly a bright light shone down from heaven and an angel appeared to us and began to speak. At first I trembled with fear at the wondrous sight, but the angel said, 'Do not be afraid,' and my fear was gone. 'Close by,' said the angel, 'in the little town of Bethlehem, a child is born. His name will be called Jesus, the Son of the Most High God. He has come to offer peace and joy to everyone. Just follow that bright new star. . . .' As the angel pointed to the heavens, I saw a brilliant star I had never seen before, just above the town of Bethlehem.

"I was so anxious to see this child, the Son of God, that I tumbled down the hill and ran all the way to Bethlehem. I searched everywhere, but all the inns were full. No new travelers had been taken in that night. By the time I reached the last inn, I was very discouraged and ready to go back to the fields. But as I knocked on the door, I felt a wave of encouragement because the bright star seemed to shine just a little brighter.

"'Oh, yes,' said the innkeeper, 'I really felt sorry about putting them in the stable, but I didn't have any more rooms. At least there's clean hay. . . .'

"He had barely finished his reply before I had run around to the back of the inn and found the little stable. Mary and Joseph had laid the new baby Jesus in a manger because they had no bed. When I arrived I was huffing and puffing, but no one turned to look at me: not the milk cow nor the little gray donkey; not the sheep nor the chickens; not even the old watchdog. No, everyone was just looking at the small child, the Son of God."

he littlest shepherd sat up on the rock. There was no hint of sleep left in his eyes.

"Was that the last you saw of this baby Jesus, Grandfather?"

"No, Grandson. It just so happened that in those days the grass was greener and the country was safer to the north, so my father and I led our flock up to Nazareth. I later came to find out that the baby Jesus and His family had also moved to Nazareth, and I was very excited.

remember one day Jesus came out to the field where we were tending the flock. We sat in the grass and ate lunch and Jesus told many wonderful stories. He was a fine storyteller, and each one He told seemed to contain a message. To my surprise, He knew more about caring for sheep than I did.

"J esus also became a good carpenter. As a helper to His father, He made some of the most beautiful pieces of furniture J had ever seen. Every piece He made was special to Him—just like the people around Him. Everything He created was a little different from all the rest, and had its own special purpose.

"Once He made me a new shepherd's staff, and I've had it ever since." With that the eldest shepherd held up his staff in his right hand for the littlest shepherd to see. "Its wood is so smooth and strong . . . and it is perfectly balanced and weighted. He made it just for me, and since then it has been the only one I have ever needed."

he eldest shepherd set the staff down and continued his story.

"When He had grown to be a man, He began to do miracles. I have seen Jesus heal the sick, make the blind to see, cause the lame to walk, and even raise the dead. Why, one day I even saw Him feed more than five thousand people with only five loaves of bread and two small fish—and then have many baskets of food left over after the meal!"

"But how can a man do miracles?" the littlest shepherd wondered.

"Because He was not just a man," answered his grandfather. "He was the Son of God."

The littlest shepherd nodded his head.

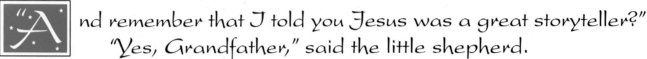"And remember that I told you Jesus was a great storyteller?"

"Yes, Grandfather," said the little shepherd.

"In those days He began to speak across the countryside, and large crowds of people began to follow Him wherever He went. He would speak to them in parables—simple stories that had a deeper meaning. In these parables, Jesus spoke to the people about how to live their lives and become close to God, our Heavenly Father.

"But there were some men—priests and Pharisees—who were jealous of the people's love for Jesus. These men were greedy for power, and wanted the crowds that followed Jesus to follow them instead. They began to spread lies and rumors about the Lord, and eventually made plans to have Him killed. They said Jesus deserved to die because He claimed to be the Son of God, and they were very afraid of Him.

"They hated Him so much they finally nailed Him to a cross between two criminals. They thought they had seen the last of this Jesus. But they didn't realize His death was all part of God's plan.

"Grandson, when I saw them take the body of Jesus down from the cross, I was so sorry, not only because I had lost a friend, but also because the world had chosen to turn its back on God's own Son.

"T" hen came the happiest day of my life! One of my friends told me Jesus had risen from the dead. At first I couldn't believe it, but we ran as fast as we could to the tomb to see if it was true. When I saw that the stone had been rolled away, I was overjoyed! Jesus was alive!

"I saw Him several times before He finally went back to heaven. On that last day, as Jesus went up into the clouds, He told those of us gathered there to go into all the world and tell everyone His story. After Jesus had disappeared from view, an angel came and said, 'Why are you still staring at the sky?' The angel told us to watch and be ready, because in the same way Jesus was taken into heaven, He would someday come again.

"Now, Grandson, do you understand why you must not sleep while you're watching the sheep?"

The boy thought for a moment. "Yes, Grandfather, I think I do. We have to stay awake not only to watch the sheep, but to watch for the time when Jesus Christ, the Son of God, will come again."

"You have learned a great lesson tonight," said the eldest and wisest of shepherds, with a smile.

The littlest shepherd settled himself down for the night and thought about all he had learned that day.

And he watched. . . .

And he waited. . . .

One Last Word . . .

For as long as he lived—until he, too, was old and wise—the littlest shepherd remembered to tell others the story of Jesus. This message, though of greatest importance to you and me, is simple. It can be summed up in just five words:

ACCEPT the Lord.

Accepting the Lord as our Savior means receiving forgiveness of sins through Jesus' blood on the cross.

"If you confess with your mouth, 'Jesus is Lord,' and believe in your heart that God raised him from the dead, you will be saved" (Romans 10:9).

LOVE the Lord.

After receiving Christ, He becomes our first love. The test of a first love relationship is, in time of need, who do we turn to first?

"Love the Lord your God with all your heart and with all your soul and with all your strength" (Deuteronomy 6:5).

OBEY the Lord.

To walk closely with the Lord Jesus, we must follow His guidelines for our lives written in His Word, the Bible.

"If you love me, you will obey what I command" (John 14:15).